How to Draw
CARTOONS

Adam Clay

ARCTURUS

Arcturus

This edition published in 2014 by Arcturus Publishing Limited
26/27 Bickels Yard, 151–153 Bermondsey Street,
London SE1 3HA

ISBN: 978-1-84837-495-9
CH001327UK

Author and illustrator: Adam Clay
Editor: Fiona Tulloch
Design and layout: Gary Sutherland
Cover design: Beatriz Reis Custodio

Picture credits:
Alamy: p6 bottom, p8 bottom
Kobal Collection: p7 top left and bottom
Mary Evans: p6 top
Rex: p6 middle, p7 top right, p8 top

Supplier 26, Date 0414, Print run 3308

Printed in China

Contents

Introduction

Hi, I'm Adam Clay and I'll be your host for this book! I'll show you how to draw excellent cartoons all of your own.

Step-by-step drawings

I'll show you how to draw things such as people and animals using simple four-step diagrams. I'll use blue and red for the first few steps so that you can clearly see what to do. When you draw the pictures yourself, don't use red and blue pencil crayons, as these don't rub out! Just use a normal lead pencil.

Step 1 shows you how to sketch the rough outline of your figure; lines are shown in blue.

Step 2 gives more definition to your rough shapes and adds detail; lines are shown in red, over the top of the blue lines.

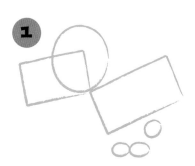

Step 3 shows the finished inked drawing, with all the detail in place; these lines are black. All blue and red lines are rubbed out.

Step 4 is the final colour drawing. Your cartoon is complete!

The right tools

I like to use a hard pencil (H or 2H) for my initial sketches and a softer pencil (HB or 2B) for adding more detail.

Pencil crayons, marker pens or felt tips are great for colouring cartoons. Watercolour paint can also give a really nice effect but remember to use fairly thick paper to soak up the water. If you're a geek like me you could even try scanning your drawings and colouring them up on the computer!

2B, or not 2B... that is the question!

Finding your own style

You may have heard it before, but it's true that everyone has their own unique style of drawing. And so do you – even if you don't know it yet! This book will give you lots of helpful hints, but it's important to develop your own drawing style as you go through the book. This will create the magic 'individuality factor' which will make your artwork exciting and unique.

I'll be giving you exercises throughout this book such as changing figures, dressing characters and adding finishing touches to scenes, to help you develop your own style.

You'll be dressing this chap on p50!

You'll be transforming this princess into an evil witch on p59!

A history

Before you start drawing your own cartoons, it's good to learn when they came about and why some characters have remained popular from their creation to today.

Felix the Cat (right) was popular in the silent film era of the 1920s. He was drawn very simply and his body and face were very adaptable, allowing for highly exaggerated expressions and movements.

The Belgian artist *Hergé* created *Tin-Tin* (left), a young, adventurous reporter, for a comic strip in 1929. Hergé drew his characters with quite a lot of detail and gave them good action poses.

Peanuts (below) was created in 1950 by Charles M. Schulz for a newspaper comic strip and remained in print for 50 years! The characters were simple in their construction but were still expressive – Schulz developed a style that worked for both printed cartoons and moving animation. *Peanuts* marked the start of cartoons moving from print to TV and film.

Modern cartoons

During the 1930s and 1940s Warner Brothers Studios made short cartoons for the cinema featuring characters such as *Daffy Duck* and *Bugs Bunny*. These characters combined animal features with human characteristics and expressions. This became a very familiar style of cartoon, and Warner Brothers animations were viewed on TV around the world.

Television animation became more popular when people began buying their own TVs. During the 1950s and 1960s, animation studios like Hanna-Barbera developed a range of popular characters and shows such as *The Flintstones*, *The Jetsons* and *Yogi Bear*.

Today's most popular characters are those who are immediately recognisable and distinctive, such as *Spongebob* and *The Simpsons*. Matt Groening, creator of *The Simpsons*, believes "the great, memorable characters in cartoons are the ones you can identify in silhouette". Think about it yourself...could you recognise Homer Simpson from just his shadow? You probably could!

Japanese Cartoons

Manga and *anime* are the terms for the Japanese comics and cartoons that became popular in Europe and the USA in the 1950s. The Japanese cartooning style uses realistic body proportions, but the faces are simplified so that they can show very exaggerated expressions. Common features are large eyes, small mouths, tiny noses and spiky hair, as seen on *Astro Boy* (right). More detailed *anime* characters appear in animated movies, whereas simplified characters appear in cartoon TV shows.

Have a Go!

When drawing your own cartoons, it's a good idea to add elements from your favourite characters into your own drawings, whether they come from video games, CGI (computer-generated imagery), traditional animation, or comics. Use those characters as a source of inspiration, and then create something new of your own. Even experienced cartoonists and animators sketch and scribble new ideas, taking inspiration from around the world to keep their work exciting and interesting. If you keep experimenting and practising, maybe you could be a cartoonist or an animator of the future!

Drawing People

Hey, who are you calling simple?!

Ok let's start with the basics! Cartoons can look quite complicated, but the truth is that once you understand each step you need to take to draw them, it all becomes quite simple.

In this chapter, you'll learn to piece together your characters using basic geometric shapes: squares, circles, triangles and ovals. Once you get a feel for it, you'll quickly learn to put your drawings together. So turn the page to get started!

Sometimes cartoons can be quite lifelike!

When drawing cartoon characters, it makes sense to start from the top! The head is the key feature of any cartoon character.

Here are some basic shapes you can use when drawing cartoon heads. Notice how different the shapes look once the features are in place.

A rectangle gives a long, thin head. This is good for tall characters.

An oval gives a soft shape. This is good for gentle and young characters.

A triangle gives a quirky, angular head. This is good for funny characters.

Single-shaped heads, the type used in these examples, make characters distinctive and appealing, but are fairly one-dimensional.

Drawing the head using two shapes instead of one makes characters more adaptable and easier to draw from different angles. Think of the top shape as the skull and the bottom part as the jaw. There are lots of possible combinations.

oval + triangle

circle +
rectangle

oval + oval

circle + oval

Try a few combinations of your own and don't be scared to try something wacky!

Eyes are the most expressive feature of all cartoon characters. They don't have to be detailed though – some of the most effective cartoon eyes are the simplest.

The most common shapes for cartoon eyes are ovals or circles, but it's fun to experiment with other shapes. Adding eyelids, altering the angle of the eyebrows and changing the size of the pupil helps to create different effects.

The angle of the eyebrows is always important when drawing cartoon eyes. Bringing down the level of the eyebrows to obscure part of the eye will help to portray grumpy, angry, concentrating or determined characters.

The main difference between male and female cartoon eyes is the addition of eyelashes. These can be drawn to look realistic, comical, or glamorous.

Try experimenting with different eye shapes, pupil sizes and eyelid widths. It's always good to vary eyes across different characters, but you'll probably adopt a few 'favourites' that you'll use more than any others.

Think about how often you use your mouth every day. Cartoon characters are just the same!

A character can have a tiny upturned mouth in one frame then a huge beaming smile in the next. The most interesting characters are those that show a wide range of different emotions. Getting the mouth right is vital when creating mood and personality.

Here are a few examples that show how simply mouths can be drawn. Sometimes a simple line or circle is all that's needed.

At other times, you might want to make the mouth expression clearer by showing teeth. A smile with lots of teeth looks cheesy, while a toothy grimace is more menacing than a frown.

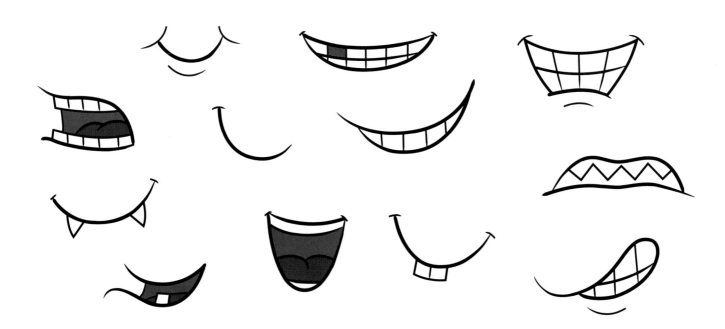

Lips are also useful when drawing fish!

Female characters are sometimes shown with full lips to add shape and colour to their faces.

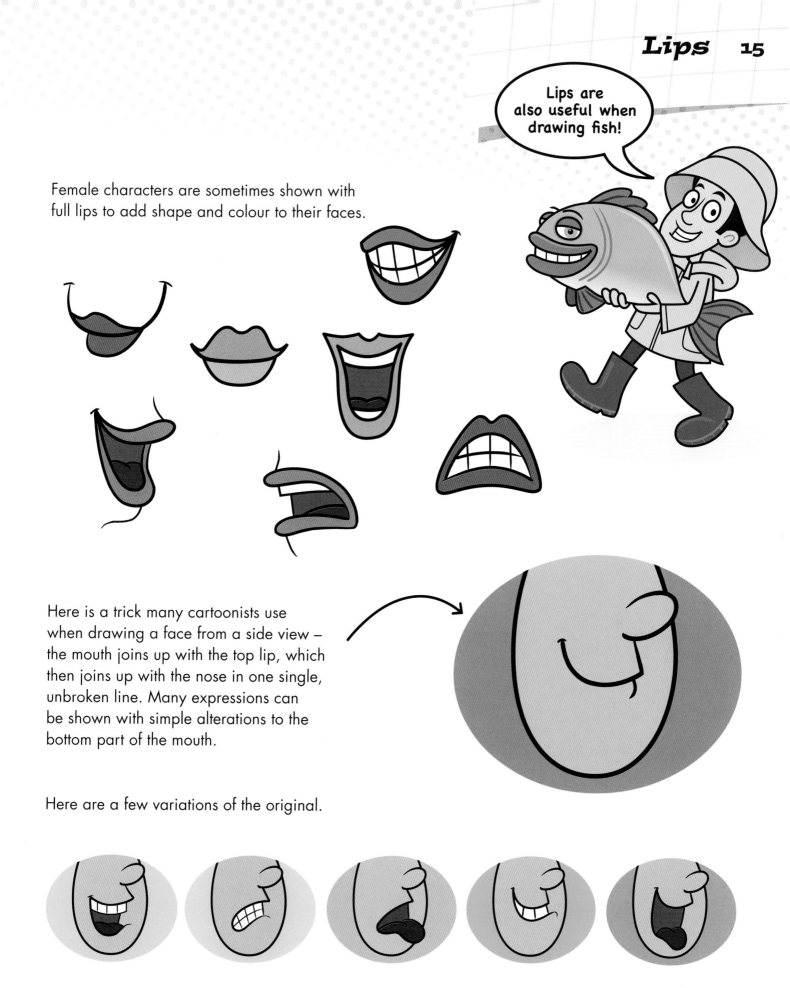

Here is a trick many cartoonists use when drawing a face from a side view – the mouth joins up with the top lip, which then joins up with the nose in one single, unbroken line. Many expressions can be shown with simple alterations to the bottom part of the mouth.

Here are a few variations of the original.

A simple curved line is often all you need in order to illustrate a nose. Here are a few simple examples.

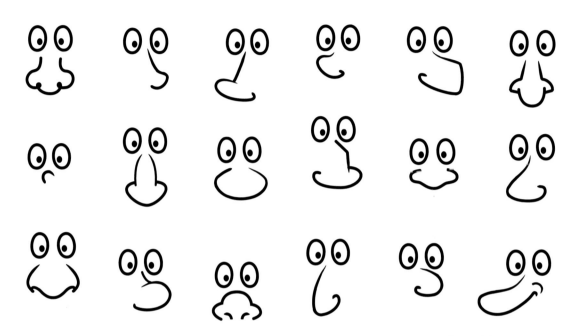

Nose shapes become the focus of a face when that character has facial hair. Here are some typical cartoon beards and noses.

Thin   Bushy   Detective   Handlebar

Hairy   Chinese   Goatee   Long
           emperor

Now it's time to think about where to place the features on the face.

Everyone knows that the eyes go at the top, the mouth at the bottom and nose somewhere in between. But that still gives us quite a lot of flexibility!

It's useful to think about a face as having gridlines, like this.

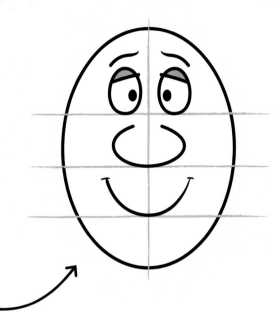

Here are a few examples that show different effects. The shape of the face and features are all the same, but I've varied the size and where I've put them.

Large eyes placed towards the bottom of the face create a cute, innocent look. Moving the mouth up to leave a large chin area at the bottom of the face can make a character appear more masculine.

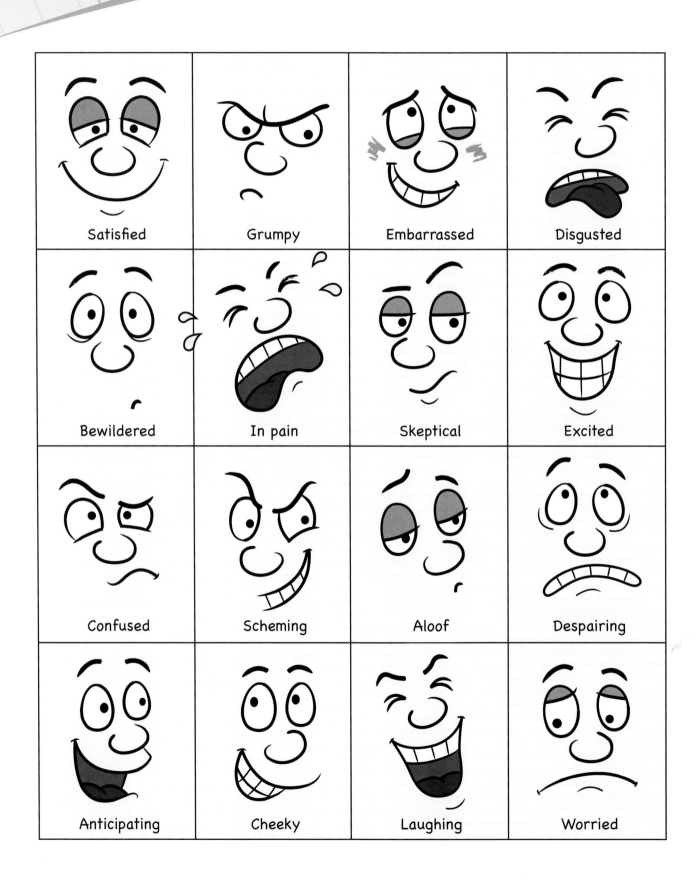

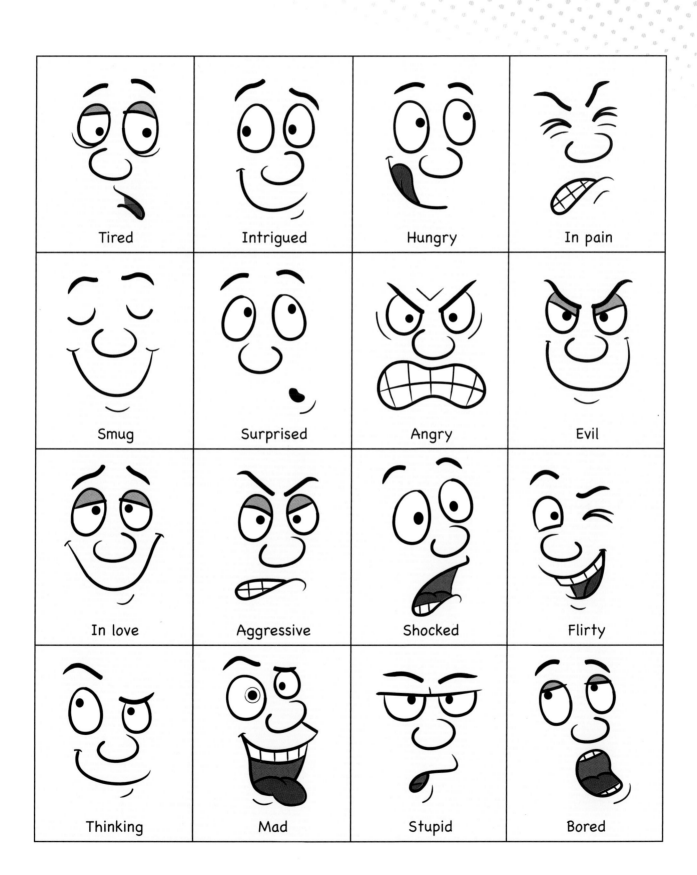

Tired · Intrigued · Hungry · In pain

Smug · Surprised · Angry · Evil

In love · Aggressive · Shocked · Flirty

Thinking · Mad · Stupid · Bored

When drawing cartoon hair, it's important to keep things as simple as possible.

Trying to draw hair in a realistic way can be tricky as it is made up of lots of individual strands. Instead, think of hair as one single shape. This will make it easier to draw, which is handy if you will be drawing the same character more than once.

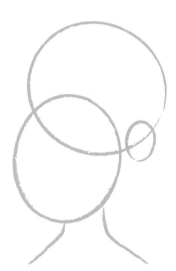  

1 Start with your basic head shape (see p10–11).

2 Add the facial features and hair outline (see p17).

3 Draw the features and give the hair a ruffled edge to make it look more realistic.

Men usually have short hair so it's good to practise some different styles so that your characters have their own individual look.

Another tip for drawing hair is to draw the hairstyle of someone you know. Copy the basic shape and form then add extra detail to make it look more distinctive or humorous. Here's a sketch of my friend Katie!

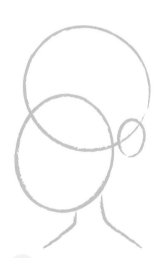  

1 She has a round face and thick hair, so I've used two round shapes.

2 She has large eyes and her hair is thickest at the top and sides of her face.

3 I've added flicks at the bottom and separated some strands of her fringe.

Hair can be as detailed or as simple as you like depending on the style of your character. Remember that ladies like to tie their hair up occasionally too!

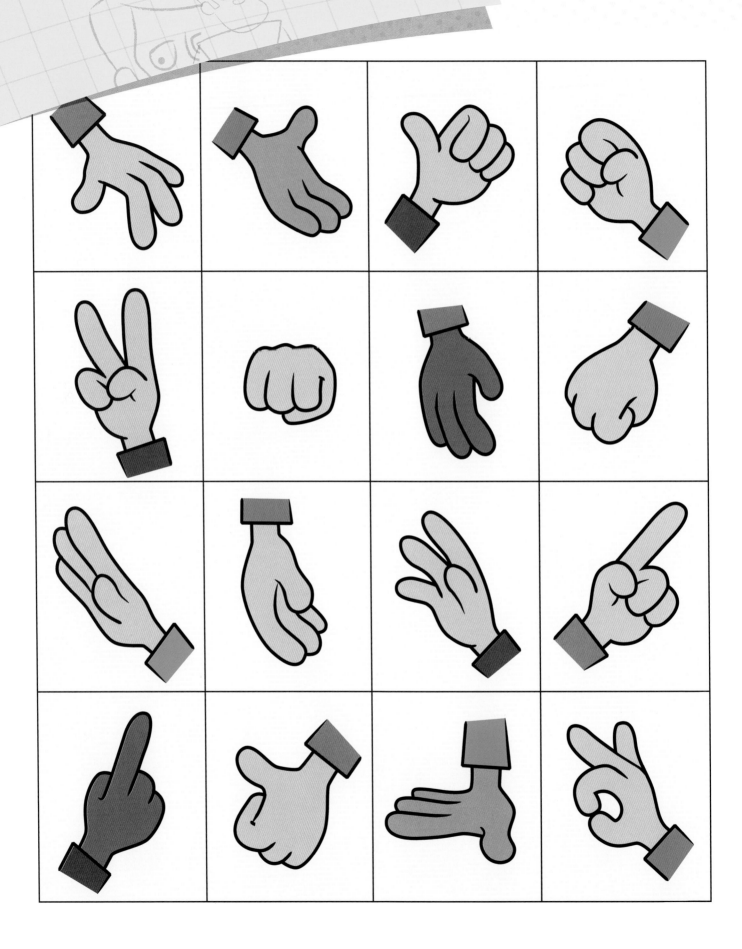

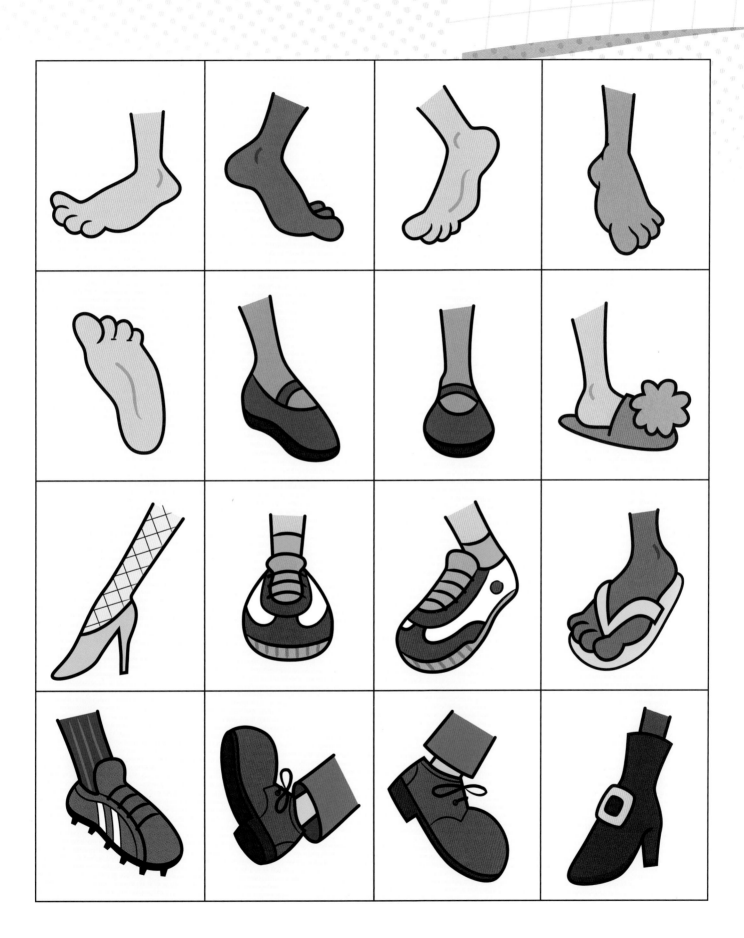

Why draw five fingers when four will do?!

Cartoonists often like to cheat and draw hands with only three fingers and a thumb. I find that normal five-fingered hands can look a little overcomplicated in comparison to the rest of the drawing. It's strange but true! The style and shape of the hands can be specific to your character.

Here are a few simple variations.

Typical cartoon hand

The basic hand with even fingers. This is the hand I usually start with before adapting it to suit the character.

Stocky hand

A square, angular hand Can be useful for strong or brutish characters.

Child's hand

Short, fat fingers and a wide wrist. A scaled up version of this could be used for a chubby adult!

Wacky hand

Long, ballooning fingers and a small palm area. This is a more 'cartoony' look, useful for comical characters.

Lady's hand

Slender, pointy fingers and a narrow wrist. A bonier version of this could also be used for a creepy villain!

Now you've learnt some of the basics, it's time to put them together to create some characters of your own!

Choosing the body shape of your cartoon character is important, as all the other features are laid on top of this initial drawing. I like to 'build' the shape of my characters using simple geometric shapes.

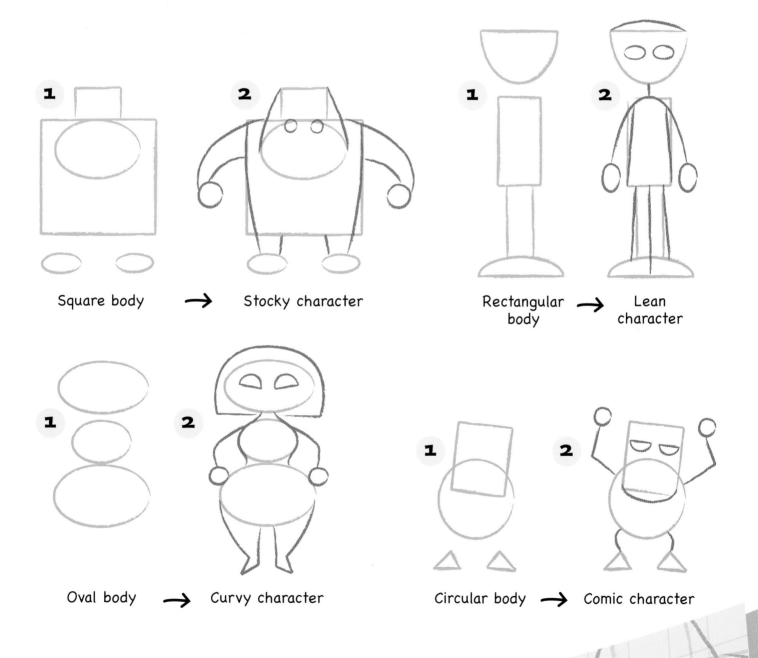

Square body → Stocky character

Rectangular body → Lean character

Oval body → Curvy character

Circular body → Comic character

Once you have your basic body form, your characters can really start taking shape.

To create your characters, take your initial sketch then add detail in pencil, finish with ink, then add colour. Here's an example of a prince charming character.

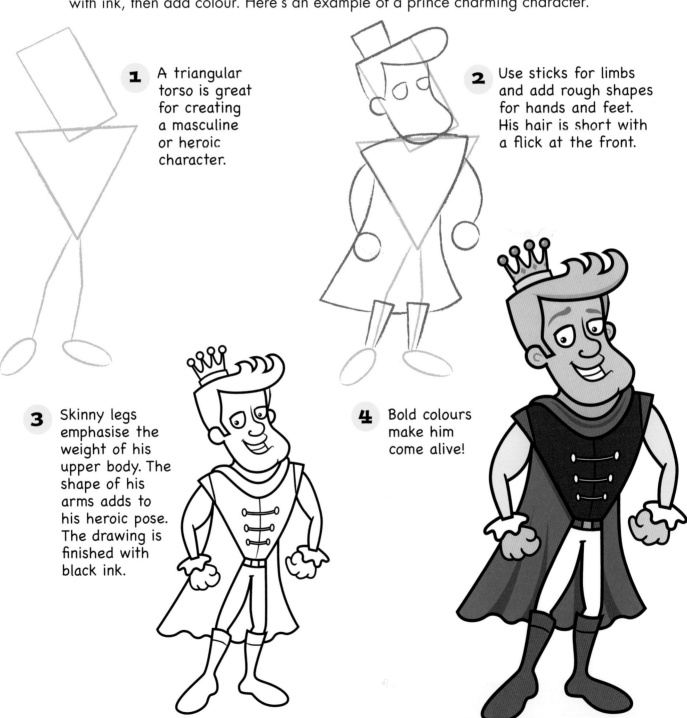

1 A triangular torso is great for creating a masculine or heroic character.

2 Use sticks for limbs and add rough shapes for hands and feet. His hair is short with a flick at the front.

3 Skinny legs emphasise the weight of his upper body. The shape of his arms adds to his heroic pose. The drawing is finished with black ink.

4 Bold colours make him come alive!

Now let's use the techniques we've learned to create a couple of other characters. I'm going to draw a brother and sister, so I'll keep the basic proportions similar but include some variation of shape to make the pair more visually interesting.

Fun seaside details complete the scene. Notice how the position of the hands helps to add expression to the characters. She's not happy!

Meet Mr Underpants! He's looking a little lost here, don't you think? We'll be dressing him up later, but for now let me show you how I've created this dopey looking character!

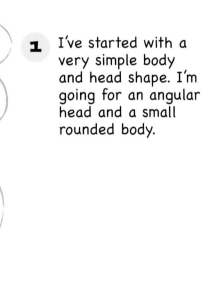

1 I've started with a very simple body and head shape. I'm going for an angular head and a small rounded body.

2 Next, I'll add the legs and arms. This is a partial side view, so only part of his left arm is showing. Bent legs give him a relaxed posture.

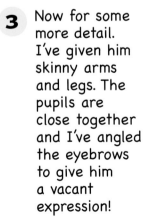

3 Now for some more detail. I've given him skinny arms and legs. The pupils are close together and I've angled the eyebrows to give him a vacant expression!

4 I've finished him off with some colour... including some tired old green underpants!

Turn to p50 if you want to dress him immediately!

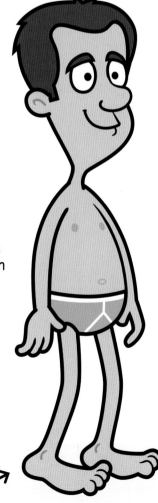

Animal Antics

Some people think that drawing cartoon animals is more difficult than drawing cartoon people. Actually, they are just as easy and can be drawn using the same principles.

The next few pages will show you some simple, fun ways to draw birds, pets, wild animals and other cartoon favourites in easy step-by-step drawings. It's so easy to draw animals that you'll forget you ever found it difficult!

Speak for yourself – I never forget anything!

The first rule to remember when drawing animals is that they are not direct copies of real animals! We alter their proportions and give them human characteristics to add humour.

Drawing birds is fun because it's easy to create different types of bird by making just a few alterations to the shape of the body, head and beak. Leave the feathers until the end when the basic shapes are all in place. Try this bald eagle for starters.

The eagle is the boss of the cartoon bird world! His square head and furrowed brow suggest that he is a determined, brave and mean character. The neck is thicker than with other birds and the head is quite square.

Ducks are naturally funny creatures and are great fun to draw. For step 1, keep the head fairly small and leave space for the neck. Add a large flat beak and big flat feet in step 2, then finish off with the face and feathery detail.

Parrots are very distinctive – they have a large curved beak with a pointed end and a long feathered tail. Bright colours are also essential. You can really go wild when it comes to colouring a parrot!

Many animals are drawn using the same building blocks. These are usually round shapes, such as circles and ovals.

This cartoon rabbit and squirrel have lots of features in common. The main difference is in the size of the legs, feet and ears.

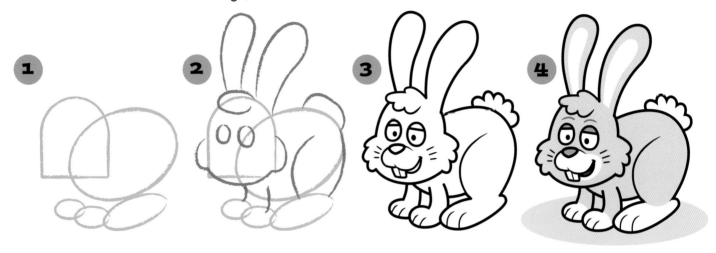

Start with a large shape for the rabbit's head. As with people, having a large head in relation to the body makes an animal look cute. Use lots of curves and avoid pointed edges. Rabbits and hares have large back legs and enormous back feet but a hare has a longer face and a less chubby body.

Cartoon squirrels are quick-witted, mischievous characters. Give them rounded cheeks and pointed ears. In these examples I've drawn a crouching rabbit and a standing squirrel, although it would be fine to draw them the other way around.

Snakes are often portrayed as villainous or sinister characters in cartoons, but a silly snake can be just as entertaining!

Draw the snake using three ovals of different sizes to represent the coiled body. Rub out some of the inner lines as shown in step 2 and draw in the facial detail and pointed tail. Finally, give your snake a zigzag pattern to warn of danger!

Keep the lines of a reptile's body round and not too angular. This lizard has distinctive toe shapes and large round eyes on the top of his head.

Cats are fun to draw! There are many different ways to illustrate them. Here are just a few.

Here's a slinky character. A slender body, large, leaf-shaped eyes and a small nose give this Siamese cat her feminine charm. I often enlarge cartoon feet to add humour, but these feet are a fairly realistic size which helps to give her an air of refinement.

A walking cat can be tricky to get right. Have a look at a photo of a real cat or use this example as a guide, then experiment with different head, body and foot shapes.

A kitten always has a large head and a small body. In cartoons they are usually drawn sitting down, similar to the rabbit on p32, but with the head held up higher. Cats usually have an arched back even when sitting down.

When drawing animals, cartoonists sometimes adapt them to make them appear more human. The (very long) word that we use to describe this is *anthropomorphism*.

Take this ginger cat for example – he is standing on two legs and is wearing a t-shirt. He looks like a real person! When animals look like people, you can draw them looking happy, sad, running, talking, waving…lots more things than when they look realistic.

Cartoonists always enjoy drawing dogs! There are lots of different breeds, so you can experiment with different shapes and sizes for your building blocks.

The sitting position for a dog is similar to that of a cat or other mammals, but the main variation is in the line of the back. I've used a combination of two shapes in step 1 to show the difference. Half closed eyelids give this chap a dopey expression and a large tongue is always funny!

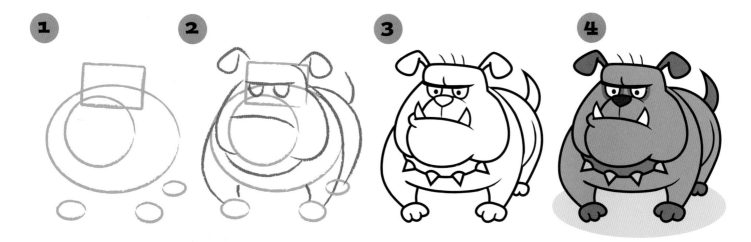

Here's a character you wouldn't want to mess with: the bulldog. He's broad, stocky and mean and not the brightest hound in the pound! When drawing heavier characters it's useful to keep the legs wide apart. This helps to spread the weight. Give him a large lower jaw and small eyes that are close together.

Cartoon dogs are often loyal, eager and enthusiastic and are usually drawn running around a scene causing mischief! Here's a dog in a running pose which looks speedy and dynamic.

Start with a circle for the head and a rectangle for the body. The body should be at an angle so that the rear end is in the air. Next, add the nose and legs. Some floppy ears and a tongue flying backwards help to create a sense of movement.

We'll cover some of these movement symbols on p78–81.

Finally, add a puff of smoke and some action lines and there you have it – a heroic, speedy mutt on his way to save the day…or maybe not!

Farmyard animals are always expressive and their emotions are easy to read. Cows, pigs and mice are farmyard favourites.

Cows have fairly square bodies compared to other animals. This example starts with a rectangle and ovals for the head and nose.

I've added eyelashes and curly hair to show that this cow is female. Her legs are quite thin which looks funny because she is so big! You can colour your cow in various ways. I've gone for the Friesian variety here, which is white with black markings.

You'll rarely see a skinny pig in cartooning! They are always chubby, rounded characters with short legs.

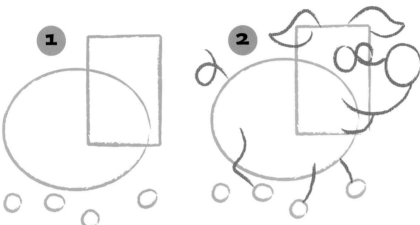

Start off with a large, round body then add a square for the head. Once you're happy with the head and body shapes, it's a good idea to blend the two together to remove any suggestion of a neck. Rather than a flat-ended snout, I tend to use a banana-shaped snout to make it look even more comical.

This mouse has an upright standing pose, with the legs blending into the sides of the body rather than coming off the bottom. This trick is useful when drawing standing animals. Draw small animals as simply as possible.

It's a good idea to do some research when drawing cartoon animals. You can find animal pictures easily in books or on the internet (as long as you have a parent to help you).

Running horses can be quite tricky to draw, so I've found a good photograph which I'm going to use.

I don't want to copy the photo and create a realistic drawing. Instead, I'll just take the key features and use them to make my cartoon version more accurate.

I've shortened the length of the body and enlarged the head for cartoon effect. The legs are in a similar position to those in the photograph. (Horses' legs can be tricky to get right so this photo is really useful for reference.)

Here's the final drawing. As you can see I've used the same colours but some features are clearly different from the photograph. The mane is fuller, the legs are skinnier, the feet are larger...and I have never seen a real horse with such a cheesy grin!

Once you're happy with the drawing, you can adapt it to create different types of animal. A few simple alterations can turn a horse into a unicorn or even a zebra!

Over the next few pages I'll give you some tips on drawing wild animals. Their body shapes make them good fun to draw!

This is a typical cartoon lion – powerful, strong and rather grouchy! Most of the weight is concentrated around the front of the body; you can see this from the low down from paws in step 1. This big cat has legs similar to his domestic cousins but the head shape is quite different. Try removing the mane and softening the eyes for a female version.

Now here's a less fearsome fur ball! When drawing young lions and tigers keep the legs chunky Cat the body rounded. Cubs should be energetic and adventurous, so wide eyes and eager expressions work well.

Cartoon dolphins are really easy to draw. The body shape is very basic and their main distinctive feature is the shape of the nose and mouth. Dolphins can be drawn in any position as they leap out of the water at lots of different angles.

Fish come in many shapes and sizes but they are also very simple to draw. Here are some sketches to give you some ideas. Vary the shape and size of the body and tail, then add the face and fins.

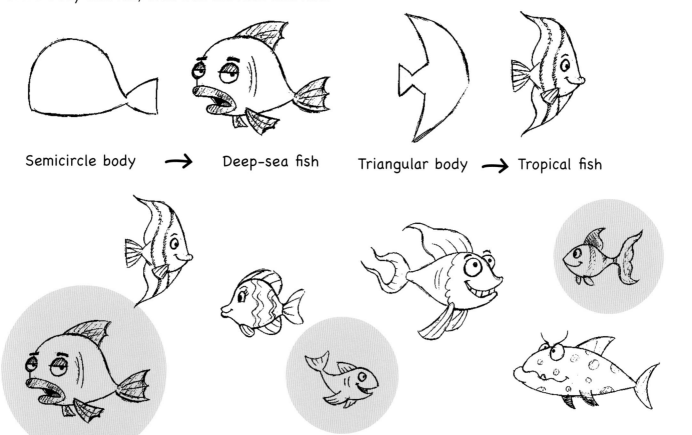

Semicircle body → Deep-sea fish   Triangular body → Tropical fish

1

2

3

For a good bear shape, think of a pear! It will concentrate the weight around the lower part of the body. Bears can be drawn standing, or on all fours, but they always have a fairly large bottom!

When you draw the arms, position them halfway down, leaving a gap below the head. Make the paws large and heavy-looking. Draw the legs bending at the knee with some distance in between them so that they support the bulky frame.

Bears are great fun to draw as their faces are so expressive, like human faces. See p122–123 for tips on facial expressions.

4

This cartoon elephant is basically just a big oval on legs! The legs are shaped like pillars, holding the weight of the body. Elephants have thick wrinkled skin, but a few lines on the knees and trunk are all you need to give this impression.

The trunk and the ears are probably the trickiest parts to get right. In this example, the trunk acts as the top lip and links with the bottom part of the mouth. The ears sit high on the head and stick out like wings.

Happy lion

Proud mouse

Hard-working beaver

Miserable tortoise

Upset penguin

Cheeky spider

Annoyed bear

Laughing fox

Adoring chimp

Happy chimp

Jealous gorilla

Cartoon animals are much more interesting when we give them human emotions or make them perform human actions. Try to give them their own personalities as I've done here in this birthday party scene!

You can create cartoon animals and people using the same basic shapes – you build your characters using simple geometric shapes then finish with detail and colour at the end.

As a final exercise, try copying the basic building blocks of this scene below, but change the man's clothing and the breed of dog to something of your choice.

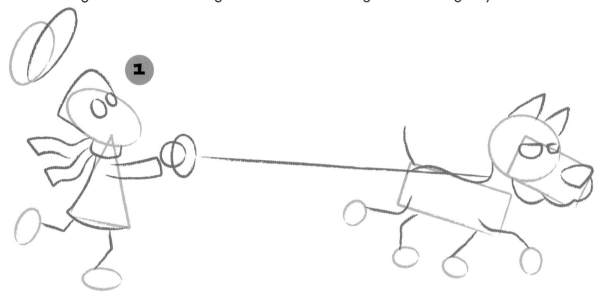

Here's my finished cartoon. You could find some pictures of other dog breeds to copy or even try reducing the size of your dog for added comedy effect!

Developing Characters

Now that we've covered the basics of drawing cartoon people and animals, it's time to think more about developing individual characters.

Details such as body shape, facial features, costumes and accessories are all vital ingredients that combine to create interesting and memorable cartoon characters. In this chapter you'll learn about those all-important details that will bring your creations to life!

Whoa, totally right-on dude!

Here's our friend Mr Underpants. He's been waiting like this for a whole chapter so it's about time we gave him something to wear!

Choosing the right outfit and accessories can really help to make cartoon characters distinctive and recognisable. The body construction and face are always important, but the clothes also give us important information about the type of character.

I reckon this lot might give us a few ideas!

FANCY DRESS

We'll use Mr Underpants as our model. The proportions of his body and face will remain the same over the next few pages, but we'll dress him up in a range of outfits with accessories, too. You'll see that the same basic character can appear very different when we alter just their clothing and accessories.

Wizard

Pointed
hat

Grey
beard

Stars on
clothing

Cape

Magic
staff

Curled up
shoes

Vampire

Slicked back
hair

Sharp
teeth

Cape with
high collar

Bow tie

Dark suit

Pointy
shoes

Pirate

Pirate hat

Eye patch

Hooked hand

Peg leg

Knee boots

Clown

Large, bright wig

Big bow tie

Squirting flower

Braces

Short trousers

Oversized shoes

Cowboy

Space Hero

Cowboy hat

Neckerchief

Gun holster

Chaps over trousers

Waistcoat

Cowboy boots

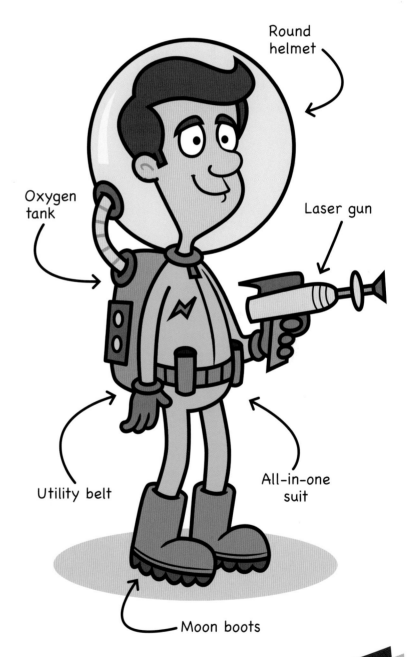

Round helmet

Oxygen tank

Laser gun

Utility belt

All-in-one suit

Moon boots

A few simple adjustments can make a big difference to the personality of a character.

Here are two similar drawings. Note how the subtle changes in costume create two totally different characters.

Round eyes

Quiffed hair

Cheesy grin

Brightly coloured outfit

Flat-ended cape

Rounded boots

This goody goody superhero is clearly flying off to save the day! His costume is bright, his features are soft and he is smiling. He's everything we expect from a superhero.

Angled eyes

Flame-like hair

Evil grin

Eye mask

Dark coloured outfit

Zigzag cape

Pointed boots

I've used the same basic pose, face and body shape here but altered a few things to turn him into a villain. Judging by his dark clothes, pointed features and evil grin, I don't think this character's flying off to save the day. He's off to cause trouble!

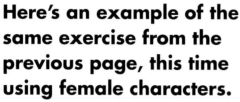

Here's an example of the same exercise from the previous page, this time using female characters.

Female characters can sometimes be tricky to draw because of their delicate features. Try copying these drawings on some sketch paper for extra practice.

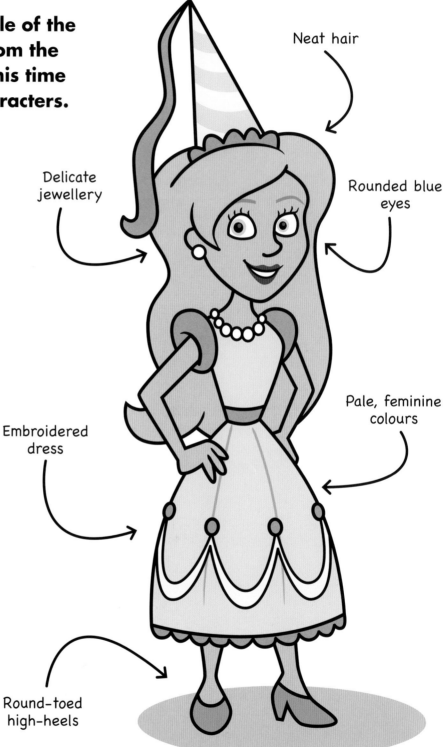

Neat hair

Rounded blue eyes

Delicate jewellery

Pale, feminine colours

Embroidered dress

Round-toed high-heels

Look at this pretty princess! Her clothes are light-coloured to suggest innocence and her facial features are large. Everything about her is rounded and delicate.

Untidy hair

Angled green eyes

Thick eye line

Hoop earrings

Shabby dress

Dark colours

Heavy shoes

Broomstick

By giving the princess's costume sharper lines and darker colours, I have created her evil witch twin! Try this exercise on some characters of your own. It's fun making a good character evil!

If you've tried drawing a character but found that they don't look quite right, it can sometimes be because they don't look the correct age.

Age can be hard to get right as there are a lot of factors involved. Here I'll show you the ageing process at double-quick speed!

Happy boy

Grumpy teenager

Child

Here's a young boy aged 7 with his whole life ahead of him. He has a large head in relation to his body. His arms and legs are short and his facial expression is lively. His clothes are bright and his t-shirt has a bold pattern.

Teenager

Now he's 15, a gangly, slouching teen. His knees are bent and his legs are long but the torso remains small in comparison. I've given him a floppy haircut which helps to define his age. He's also dressed in casual teen clothing.

Grown-up dad

Elderly Grandad

Adult

A grown-up aged 40. The upper body and arms can be much broader in fully grown adults. His head has become longer and I've given him a receding hairline and sideburns. His clothes reflect his job and are very smart.

Grandad

Now he's a wise old man of 80! The top half of his body is bent over. His ears and the nose are slightly larger and he has a long grey beard. Carpet slippers and cardigans are always a good look for oldies!

Good boy

Naughty boy

A *stereotype* is something that conforms to our idea of what we expect it to be. Stereotypes are easy to relate to and by looking at them we immediately know who they are.

With cartoons, the humour comes from being able to clearly identify characters as soon as we see them. Some of the most memorable cartoon characters are those that we understand from just a quick glance.

Before you start creating a character, scribble down a list of features you'd expect that character to have. For example, a headmistress would probably have smart clothes, tied-up hair and a stern expression. Once you have your list, choose the features you want your character to have. You should try to include at least three of the key features from your list.

The examples on these pages illustrate some common cartoon stereotypes.

Businessman

Homely mother

Spy

Surfer Dude

Sexy lady

Using the skills you've learned so far, and with a little imagination, you can create some great fantasy cartoon characters.

Ogre

Fairy

Elf

Goblin

When I draw imaginary characters or monsters, I like to experiment using different elements from humans and animals. These are some make-believe characters that often appear in cartoons.

Here's a step-by-step exercise for drawing a big hairy monster! I've combined human features with monkey features to create the character.

Colour can make a big difference. In step 3 I've coloured the monster brown, to look like Bigfoot. In step 4 I've coloured him in white, to look like a yeti. Notice how one character design can be used to create two different monsters.

As with cartoon people, cartoon monsters can be made to look good or bad with a few simple adjustments.

This friendly dragon character wouldn't hurt a fly...

Rounded ears

Rounded wings

White, rounded eyes

Wagging tail

Rounded teeth

Bright colouring

Rounded toes

...but this bad tempered beast is another story.
Don't go too close to him or you'll be toast!

Narrowed yellow eyes

Smoking Nostrils

Pointed ears

Ragged wings

Sharp teeth

Dark colouring

Pointed claws

Have you ever seen a real alien? Neither have I...so that means that we can be really creative when drawing creatures from outer space!

Have a go at this step-by-step exercise. He's a fairly odd looking creature. Give your extra-terrestrial eyes on stalks and wiggly tentacles for a look that's out of this world!

This alien looks more like a person (two eyes, arms and legs) but he's still pretty strange! Have a go at a few of your own weird and wacky alien characters.

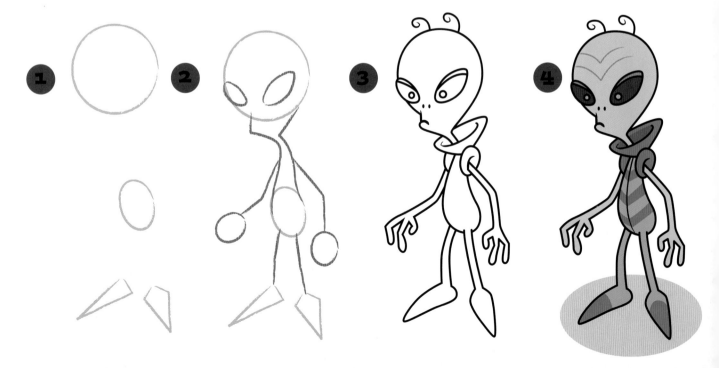

Pencils! Colour! Action!

> I've had enough of standing around...I'm outta here!

By now, you'll be able to create cartoon characters and really make them your own. But there's more to cartoons than just characters standing around... isn't there?! This next chapter will look at some of the techniques illustrators use to make their cartoons more dynamic.

We'll also tackle perspective and foreshortening as well as covering some basic movement and sports poses. Yes it's time to get your characters moving!

***Foreshortening* means drawing an object in a way that makes it look three-dimensional, even though it is drawn on a flat piece of paper. Cartoonists use foreshortening to make things in the foreground seem bigger than things in the background.**

Using foreshortening correctly can help to make your cartoons much more dramatic.

Larger foreground

Smaller background

We are looking at this girl from a high angle. As she stretches upwards, the flower and the hand that is holding it appear large in comparison to the rest of her body. Her feet are the furthest part away from us, so appear very small.

Increasing the size of things in the foreground can also add dramatic effect to action scenes. Here I've used two sporting examples to illustrate this.

The football has been enlarged so that it is as big as the player in the distance. The addition of movement lines show that the ball is moving quickly towards us.

Watch out! The boxer is swinging outwards with his fist, so I've enlarged his right glove. His left glove is behind his body so it has been reduced in size.

Foreshortening can be tricky to get right, but with a little practice it can be a very handy skill to learn. Have a go yourself.

Now it's time to think about *perspective*. Perspective describes the way cartoonists make some things look close up or far away depending on how big they are drawn on the page.

This very simplified bowling alley is really easy to draw and will show the action from an interesting angle. (This is one of the few where you might need a ruler!)

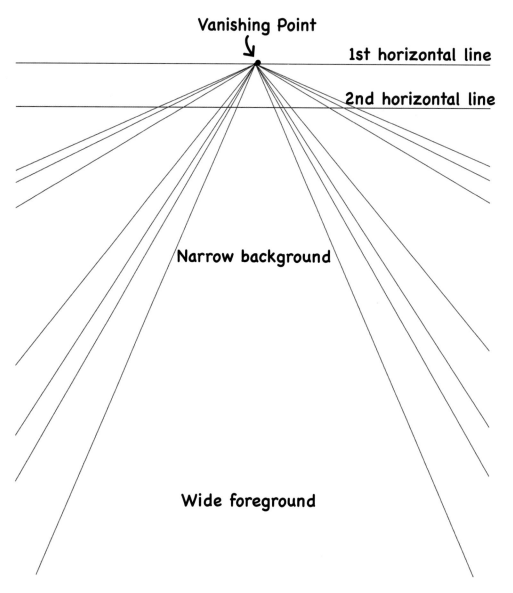

Vanishing Point

1st horizontal line

2nd horizontal line

Narrow background

Wide foreground

Start by drawing two horizontal (across) lines. Draw a dot in the middle of the first horizontal line – this will be the *vanishing point*. All of the lines on the page will go through this dot. Now draw on the lines for the bowling lanes, making sure they go through the vanishing point.

Rub out the top line, the vanishing point, and the lines above the lower horizontal line. When you are happy with the perspective you can start adding more detail.

Anything in the foreground should be much larger than things in the background. Our character at the end of the bowling lane is further away than the bowling ball and skittles, so he appears smaller in the drawing.

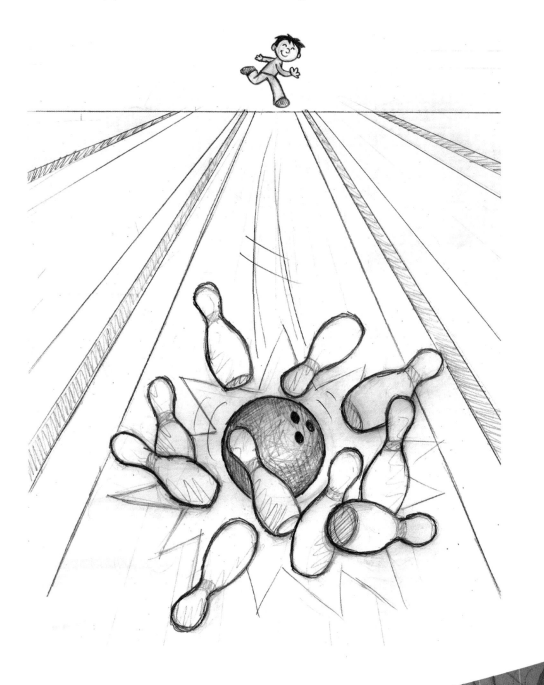

Don't put that ruler away yet! Here's another scene that follows the principles of perspective, and builds on what you've learned so far.

This time the vanishing point is off to one side instead of being in the centre. All of the horizontal lines will meet at the same spot.

Start by drawing a horizontal line then draw a dot at the far right to represent the vanishing point. Add a diagonal line from that point to show the top of the fence. (I've shaded what will be the fence area in grey.)

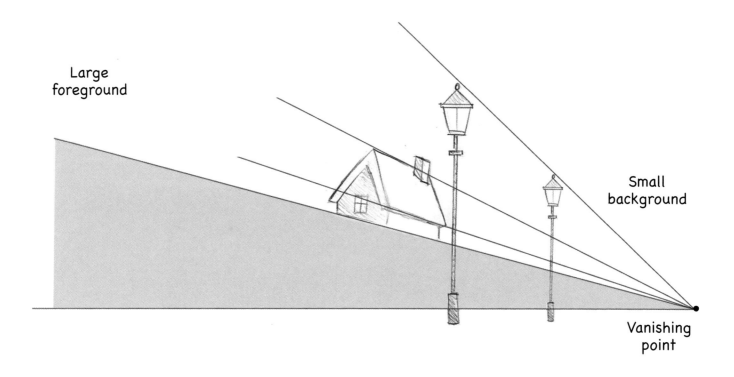

Large foreground

Small background

Vanishing point

Draw another couple of guidelines to help you to draw the roof of the house. The house is in the distance behind the fence so it will be quite small. Remember, only the horizontal lines are affected by this perspective. The vertical lines, like the lampposts, should always stay vertical!

Once you are happy with the way the drawing looks, rub out all of the guidelines and draw a series of vertical lines along the fence to represent the wooden planks. The planks should get smaller the closer you get to the vanishing point.

Add the dog and cat and any other detail you like to finish the picture.
The cat is closer to us than the dog so is slightly larger in comparison.

This leaping cat provides the action and is the part that draws the viewer's attention,
but the perspective of the background helps to make the whole scene more effective.

When a character is drawn in a strong pose, it tells us a lot about the personality or mood of the character.

Some characters have what I call 'classic poses' – certain ways of standing or gesturing that allow us to instantly recognise who or what they are.

Here are a few poses with notes on the key features.

Ballerina

- Slender limbs
- Delicate figure
- Straight legs, pointed toes
- Weight on one leg

Magician

- Feet together
- Eyes closed
- Cheesy grin
- Outstretched arms

Soul singer

- One arm outstretched
- Other hand clutching microphone
- Rounded shapes
- Wide mouth

Soldier

- Rigid posture
- Angular lines
- Legs together
- Symmetrical body

Golfer

- Legs slightly apart
- Eyes looking downwards
- Bending at the waist
- One arm bent

**Meet Bob the Slob – a chubby couch potato
in need of some exercise!**

He's so lazy –
he never moves!

Let's put him through
his paces and see what
he's made of!

"OK! Now crouch!"   "and stretch! 2, 3, 4…"   "Touch your toes…"

"and turn!"

"Now twist! 2, 3, 4..."

"and lunge! 2, 3, 4..."

"...and...rest!"

When you're developing a character to appear in a series of pictures such as a comic strip or storyboard, it's a good idea to draw them in a series of different positions and angles. This will help you to get a better idea of them as 3-D characters.

As you can see, even the most unathletic of characters can be made active with a little persuasion!

Choosing the right body position can give the appearance of a specific movement in a drawing. Adding motion lines to suggest speed can also add to the effect.

Have a look at these three body structures. They are all variations of the same basic walking position with one leg forward and one back, but they show three distinctive forms of movement.

Marching

- Straight legs
- Straight back
- Head back

Hiking

- Leaning forward
- Back leg bent
- Front leg straight

Running

- Both legs off the floor
- Arms high
- All limbs bent

Here are a few more examples to show how we use body positions and motion lines to suggest movement.

Dancing

I've gone for a fairly simple disco dance pose here. His bottom is sticking out and his arms are held away from his body, with one finger pointing. Add motion lines and musical notes to emphasize the dancing.

Jumping

This is a fairly high jump so the arms are high and the legs have swung right back behind the body. For a smaller jump the arms and legs would be lower. Again, motion lines have been added for extra effect.

Her clothes and hair are lifting up to make this look more realistic.

Waving

Show waving by adding a few small motion lines to an outstretched palm. For a bigger wave try using larger, more extreme lines.

Motion lines are a useful tool for cartoonists but can sometimes be over used. Only add them only when they are really needed to enhance a specific movement.

Here are some examples of cartoons that show sporty movements.

Sports cartoons can be tricky to get right as there is so much going on. It's best to think of your drawing as a 'snapshot' of the action. Remember, using photos for research can be very useful for drawing body positions.

Tennis

When drawing scenes with more than one character, it is a good idea to consider their different roles within the scene. This way, one player can be performing an action and another character can be anticipating or responding to it.

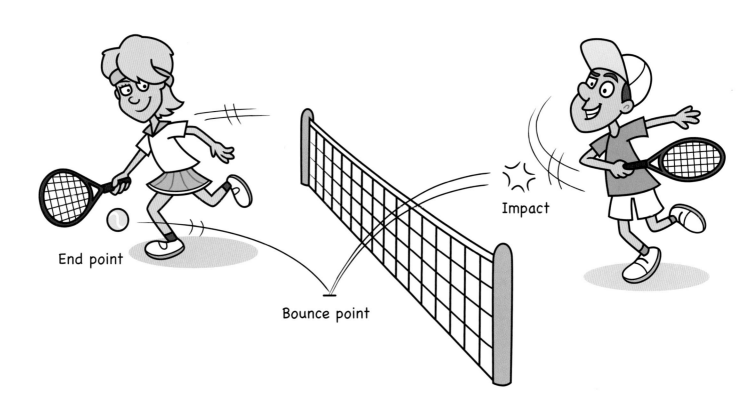

End point

Bounce point

Impact

In this tennis scene I've used a series of motion lines and effects to show the swing of the racket and the path of the ball. The body positions of the characters are essential to convey the action.

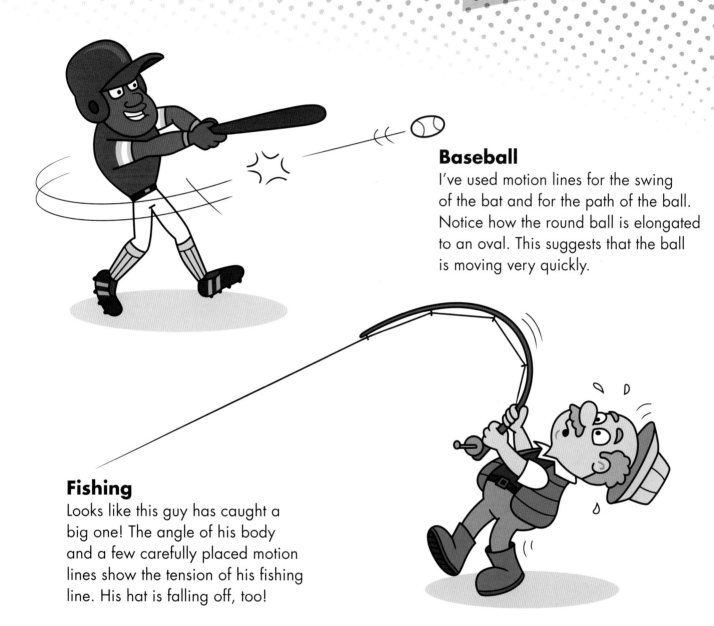

Baseball

I've used motion lines for the swing of the bat and for the path of the ball. Notice how the round ball is elongated to an oval. This suggests that the ball is moving very quickly.

Fishing

Looks like this guy has caught a big one! The angle of his body and a few carefully placed motion lines show the tension of his fishing line. His hat is falling off, too!

Swimming

Body position is all important for a swimmer. When drawing characters in water, just show a portion of their body appearing above the surface.

Cartoonists draw action lines running through the centre of a character's body to help draw the limbs and head in a way that harmonizes with the body position. They make a character's pose appear more realistic.

Here are a few small ninjas to help me explain! Start by drawing the action line itself and then gradually add the rough shapes, which will be the body structure. Rub out the action line along with your other guides before adding final detail and colour.

Think of the action line as an extension if the spine. It should be a simple sweeping line with only one or two curves. An overcomplicated action line could result in an odd-looking drawing.

With some practice you'll begin to visualise the action line in your head before starting your drawings. You may eventually find that you don't need to draw it at all.

Challenging lean

Side hand jab

Forward punch

Crouching kick

Roundhouse kick

Recoiling punch

Heavy forward punch

Use size to show the relationship between characters. Bigger characters are usually more important or more powerful than smaller characters.

Squabbling siblings

Here I've drawn a young boy being tormented by his lanky older sister! Children grow very fast so there can be big size differences in children of a similar age. I've given these characters the same hair colour to help show that they are brother and sister.

Big scary monsters

Increasing the scale of a monster or scary character can add an extra sense of menace. In this scene I've kept the girl character small even though she is in the foreground.

To make your characters more distinctive, make them different sizes and shapes – they'll stand out more than if they were all the same.

This band of pirates is constructed using different proportions for each character. We can easily identify the characters as 'the skinny one', 'the short one' and 'the big fat one'! It's a method that's really useful for making the characters memorable and immediately recognisable.

Think about how size and shape affect your characters' personalities. What are their strengths and weaknesses? In cartoons, a larger character might be physically strong, but slow-witted. A small character may be the smartest and treated as the leader or boss.

We've covered a lot in this chapter, so what better way to sum it all up than with a final cartoon!

The comic strip: analysis

In frames 2 and 4 we have a character performing an action. The movement lines and position of the body help to explain what is happening. I've placed the bald character in the foreground so that we read his expression clearly.

The character in the background is smaller in frame 2 and a bit larger in frame 4 to show he is moving towards the bald character on his chair.

By frame 5 the characters are a similar distance from the viewer. The size difference here and the position of their bodies add drama to an already tense situation!

Now that you've learned how to draw cartoon characters, it's time to create some backgrounds to really set the scene!

Here I've drawn a character standing in the middle of an empty box. Over the next few pages I'll show you how with a few simple changes, you can transform this empty box in to loads of great indoor scenes!

Where am I?

Let's start by creating a cosy living room for our character.

This scene is easy to draw. Have a look around your own living room for ideas. Rugs, curtains and cushions will create a cosy atmosphere. Draw furniture with rounded edges to make it look extra comfy, and remember that chairs and sofas often point towards the TV. Bookshelves and pictures on the walls add detail, but be careful not to overfill your scene.

Now for something a little more unusual...and creepy!

I've used dark colours here to create a spooky atmosphere. To give the impression of stone walls, outline just a few blocks around the windows and doors. Small props such as bones, chains, mice, and green slime are perfect for achieving the dungeon look and will add to the feeling of nastiness!

Here, I've given our character a job at the local supermarket.

Drawing a fully-stocked shop is not as difficult as you might think! Start by drawing empty shelves and organising the layout. Next, add all of your supermarket goods – stack the shelves with repeated images of each product. Shops usually have fairly bright lighting so keep all of the colours strong and bold.

And now for a little luxury!

This ballroom has no furniture – all the detail is in the decoration of the room, which makes it look elegant. The pillars in the corners of the room are very grand and the draped curtains add to the effect. A chandelier adds a touch of luxury and sparkle!

Enough interior decoration – it's time to go to town!

With outdoor scenes, you can make things appear as close up, or as far away as you like. Here, I've put a lot of space between the character and the buildings behind him. I've added a crossing and a fire hydrant, which both look bigger than the buildings in the Distance. If our character was standing directly outside a building, we wouldn't see much of the city at all. We have to 'zoom out' if we want to see lots of detail.

We're gone totally tropical in this jungle scene!

The secret of drawing a cartoon jungle is to keep the shapes of all the plants simple. It's best to start with the largest plants and trees, then add smaller ones to fill in the gaps. Decide which plants are in the foreground and which are in the background. Overlapping plants and trees will give the scene a sense of depth.

Uh-oh. Our character's stranded on a desert island!

Drawing a character on a tiny, deserted island makes a really funny scene!
Our man's been living here for 10 years, surviving on crabs and coconuts!
I've added just a few details to show that the island is deserted. Changing
the usual colour of things is fun to try; a sky doesn't always have to be blue!
In this scene the red sunset adds to the tropical atmosphere.

It's the future...and it's alien!

When creating landscapes for other planets, let your imagination run wild! It's fun to invent strange alien plants and choose unusual colours. Try to use colours that you wouldn't expect to see, such as the purple ground and pink plants I've used here. Craters are good for showing an undeveloped, barren moonscape. There can be all kinds of planets and stars in the sky, too.

When drawing cartoon backgrounds, start by asking yourself a few questions: What you are trying to show? What is the setting for the scene? Are you including any people?

Once you have your idea, consider the angle and distance that will give you the most effective result. Keep things simple to begin with by drawing rough shapes to represent any large structures. When you're happy with the layout, have some fun with the finishing touches. Small details give us vital information about a scene and tell us what the atmosphere is like.

Below is a simple sketch of a street. You can't tell where it is or who would live there yet.

Basic Street layout

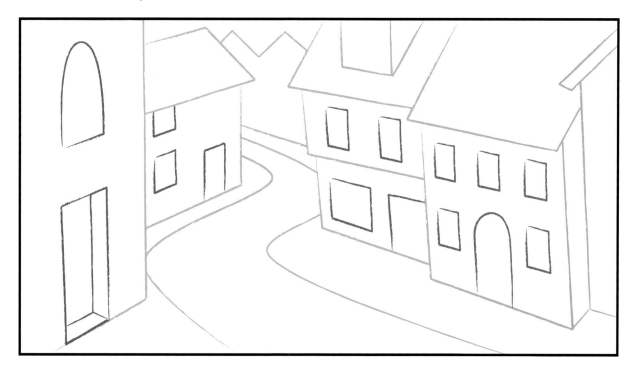

Now look at the scenes on the opposite page. With flowers under the windows, chairs in the street and bright colours everywhere, it's clear that Petunia Terrace is inhabited and vibrant. The houses are painted in warm, bright colours and yellow light behind the windows makes the place seem jolly and welcoming.

For Grimely Avenue I've stuck to a few dark colours: purple, green and grey. Broken windows and wooden boards across the windows create a dark and moody atmosphere. I know where I'd rather be! What about you?

Petunia Terrace

Grimely Avenue

Inventing cartoon buildings is really fun. Start by sketching rough shapes for the main structure of the building. Gradually add more detail until you have something you're happy with.

In the scenes on these pages, I've used the same layout position for both buildings, but changed the architecture and surroundings to create two very different atmospheres.

Fairytale castle

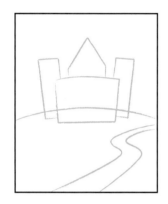

When artists draw a building in a realistic style, they use lots of straight lines. But in the world of cartoons, you can have fun creating a distorted, quirky version of reality. Try to avoid using very straight lines wherever possible to give your buildings more of a cartoony feel.

In these two scenes the vertical (straight) lines are at slightly odd angles – they're not quite straight. This adds to the overall wackiness of the buildings.

Haunted house

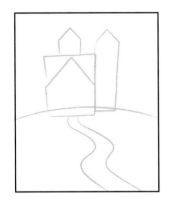

Two great ways to show distance in a scene are by using a mixture of large and small figures, overlapping the scenery.

Here I've overlapped a series of hills to create the basic landscape, then added a winding road to lead the eye from the foreground to the background. Finally, I have added a few items to show a difference in scale. The large sheep and flowers in the foreground, and the small buildings in the background, create the illusion of distance.

Country landscape

Knowing how to draw a cartoon car is essential. Every cartoon character needs a smart set of wheels!

A cartoon car is simpler and quirkier than a real one. Look at real cars for reference but don't try to copy them too closely, as it's good to give your vehicles a little personality of their own. Try this step-by-step below.

The colour of your car is as important as the style and shape!

This car is a 3-D cartoon but you could easily draw the same car from a side view. It depends how complex you want the drawing to be. The next couple of pages will show you some more cartoon vehicles drawn from a side view.

FIDO 1

Taxi

Aeroplane

Ship

Sports car

Motorbike

Stagecoach

Ice cream van

Boat

Bicycle

Truck

Train

Spaceship

Changing the way you frame your drawings makes them look even more interesting and exciting.

Peeping through a hole makes the person looking at the cartoon feel as though they are spying in some way. Here are a few examples.

Telescopic view

Keyhole view

Binocular view

Use persective to create a little drama! Here, one of the characters can't see that something dramatic is about to happen.

A sense of anticipation is great for creating comic situations. Try to draw a scene where the reader wants to shout "Look out!" at one or more of your characters.

Comic Strips

All you need is a good idea, then I'll show you how to turn it into a brilliant comic strip!

Comic strips are a great mixture of cartooning and storytelling. In this chapter you'll learn how to create your own comic strips, using all of the skills you've learned so far.

A comic strip describes a series of events using a number of panels. We'll be using a strip made of nine cells (boxes), to keep things nice and easy. Don't worry, I'll explain each step at a time!

Before you start drawing your comic strip you'll need to think about some important points:

- Who are the characters?
- Where does the action take place?
- What's the story?
- How will the characters react to each other or to a situation?

The best cartoon strips contain just a few distinctive characters that are easy to distinguish from one another. Try to think of funny situations and then think about which characters to include. Write notes in each cell as you plan. Make your story as clear as possible. Very busy scenes don't work well in small spaces!

Here's my example.

I've decided to extend the last cell by rubbing out the last gridline. This will make the final image more dramatic. At this stage, I already have an idea of the way the characters and story will look.

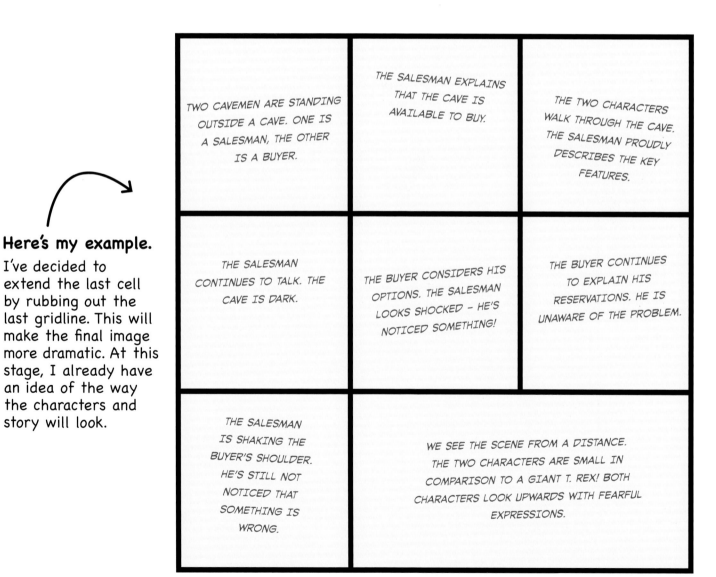

Once you've made your story notes in each cell, rub out the text and do some rough sketches of your scenes and characters. Begin with simple shapes and gradually add more detail. Remember to leave space for speech bubbles if your characters will be talking. (I'll explain about speech and thought bubbles on p114.)

You can make your comic strip more interesting by occasionally changing the reader's view. Try 'zooming in' close to your characters to show their faces, or 'zooming out' to show the scene from a distance.

When you are happy with your pencil sketches, ink over the lines, rub out
the pencil, and colour it in. (I'll give you some tips on colouring your characters
on pp126–127.) Hey presto – now you have your finished comic strip!

In the rest of this chapter I'll show you how to add special effects and
make some small changes to make your comic strips look extra special.

Where you position a character within a cell will affect how the reader sees them, reads their speech and how the background appears. Here are some good and bad examples to show you the difference.

Version 1: Bad

The problem with this cell is that the character is too far to the right. There is no space for the speech bubble in front of him so it has to go behind his head. It looks as though he's speaking out of his ear!

Version 2: Improved

Try to give your character some space in the direction they are facing, especially if they are moving. I think this cell leaves too much empty space on the right.

Version 3: Perfect!

This is the best option. There is more space in front of the character, but the cell still looks much more balanced. In this example, the speech bubble can be cut off at the corner as we only need to show two words.

Just like in the movies, your characters are actors in your story – so it's good to vary the distance of your 'shot' by zooming in or out, as I mentioned earlier.

Version 1: Full body

This version shows our character from a distance. We can see that he is grumpy by his pose, but his facial expression isn't very clear, as his face is far away. There is also a lot of empty space.

Version 2: Half body

By zooming in on the bear we see his expression more clearly. This half-body shot shows us his pose, facial expression, and the puffing smoke symbols coming from his ears. Now let's zoom in even more!

Version 3: Extreme close-up

This version creates the effect I'm looking for. His face is the focus of the cell so we can definitely tell that he is mad! This version works best because the bear's angry face is our focus – we don't need to see his pose as well. A close-up always has more impact.

Including a mixture of these three basic shots will make your cartoon strips more interesting for the reader to look at.

You can show your characters speaking and thinking by using a few different techniques.

Choosing a speech bubble depends on how many words your character will be saying and how much space there is in the cell. Generally, you should show who's speaking with a point or line coming from the speaker's mouth. The mouth should be open and the face should show an expression that matches the words being spoken.

Basic oval shape

Rounded rectangle

Partial bubble

No bubble

Thoughts and ideas are usually shown in cloud shapes. They are not spoken out loud, so there's no need to direct the shape towards the character's mouth. Instead, add a couple of small ovals between their head and the thought cloud.

Conversations

If two or more characters are speaking (or thinking) in the same cell, you will need to make it clear who is speaking first. The speech bubble for the first speaker is usually to the left and above the second speaker's bubble. This is because in our normal lives we always read from left to right, and top to bottom.

Using special effects in your cartoon strip will make some of your cells really stand out. This is very common in comic strips featuring superheroes.

I've used the super villian character I drew earlier (on p57) to show how you can make an important action scene really stand out on the page.

I've started by drawing my character and adding the special effects with simple pencil lines. I've added lightning lines to represent electric energy. Each zigzag line leads to the centre of the cell. Draw an even number of zigzag lines, so that you have an odd number of 'portions'.

I've coloured each portion of the electric energy alternately in red and yellow (this is possible because there is an odd number of portions). Both colours are lighter towards the centre of the cell to show that our villain is the source of the energy. You can easily create this effect with pencil crayons or felt tips.

Using dashes will make it look like a character is moving, or flying. The distance between the dashes gets wider as you go in the direction the character is moving. In this example, the character is flying to the left.

Notice how his hair overlaps the edge of the cell. It looks like he's bursting out of the scene!

I've coloured the background using two colours, blending them to a pale colour in the direction he's come from. Choose colours that are different to your character's clothes. This contrast will make the effect more dramatic.

Explosions are commonly used in cartoon strips and there are many ways to draw them.

When something explodes, the energy starts in the middle and moves outwards. You can use lots of different shapes to show this effect, as in these examples.

Colour is also important for drawing explosions. Use bright tones: red, orange, yellow and white are the most commonly used colours. Use lighter colours towards the centre of the explosion and darker colours around the edge.

Mushroom clouds

A 'mushroom cloud' is a big explosion that you can see from very far away, usually on land or on the sea. For an even bigger explosion, you could use a double cloud.

Fight clouds

A cloud can also be used to show a funny fight scene. Draw a cloud with arms and feet sticking out at odd angles, and a couple of stars too. It will look as though lots of people are fighting but you won't have to draw them all – easy!

Action lines around the smaller clouds make it look like the arms and legs are moving.

As well as speech, it's fun to include sounds in your comic strips. Here's where you imagination can really run wild!

When you say some words out loud, they make the sound that they are describing. This is called *onomatopoeia*. These words are great to use in cartoons. You can draw these noise words in a way that emphasises the sound they are making, too.

Sounds and noises are an important part of a cartoon strip, as they make events seem much more dramatic. You can invent any kind of noise word you like as long as it makes sense within the comic strip and is very clear.

There are no set rules about they best way to display noise words, it depends on the effect you are trying to create. For example, a noisy sheep in a field can have a large 'open' noise word (one that isn't contained inside a box), whereas an object like a telephone could have a speech bubble. Try some creations of your own and remember to be creative with the writing style too.

Silhouettes make an interesting addition to any cartoon. They are useful for setting a scene or changing a mood. A good silhouette is easy to recognise despite the lack of detail.

Draw a silhouette in the same way as any other cartoon, by starting with rough shapes and adding in the detail at a later stage. The only difference is that the final version is block coloured and any inner markings are removed. Marker pens are useful for drawing silhouettes as they create areas of solid black.

Try creating an eerie nighttime scene. Keep windows and eyes in light colours.

You can use silhouettes to create lots of easily identifiable characters in a scene that features lots of windows.

Silhouettes work well for dusk and dawn. The effect is peaceful and powerful rather than spooky.

Sometimes you don't need colour to make a cell really stand out – you can use light and shadow instead.

In this drawing of an escaped prisoner, all of the light comes from one source: a circular shaped spotlight. The area caught in the beam contrasts with the rest of the background, which is very dark. The reader understands that the area in the spotlight is the main focus of the scene.

This cartoon has a big impact despite using only two main colours.

Another common trick used by cartoonists is the 'blackout panel'. This is used to show total darkness, but still allows the reader to see where the characters are. It's a good idea to use characters with different shaped eyes, so that the reader recognises who it is within the panel.

Make sure that any speech bubbles read from top to bottom, so that they are read in the right order.

If you've created a character who will appear in your strip more than once, it's important to make sure that you are happy with the colour of their clothes and hair.

You can make copies of your characters by photocopying or tracing your original drawing, or by scanning and printing it. Once you have some blank characters, colour them in different ways to see what works best. Professional cartoonists call these tests *colour models*.

If you have created characters who will appear in the comic strip in a group, make sure that their colours work well when you put them next to each other.

Young characters are often dressed in bright, bold colours.

Villainous characters usually wear dark colours. Green and purple are particular favourites!

Once you have chosen your character colours, it's time to test out the best background colours for your scenes!

These two cells show some of the problems in colouring a scene and what you can do to make it look better.

First colour scene

- The walls are dark and too similar to the colour of the boy's hat.
- The rug and floor are both very brightly coloured which is a bit harsh on the eye.
- The boy is wearing unusual coloured trousers which looks a bit odd.
- The wooden table is the same colour as the dog.
- The colour of the chair is similar to the colour of the man's trousers and shoes.

Second colour scene

Here is what I've changed to improve the scene:

- The walls are light blue which makes the scene lighter.
- The floor is a plain dark colour which looks more natural.
- The boy is wearing 'normal' coloured clothes.
- The dog is lighter, so stands out against the brown furniture.
- The man's clothes are brightly coloured so they can be seen against the table and chair.

Here's a final comic strip to inspire you. Happy cartooning!